labournight &
other poems

Martin Connolly

labournight &
other poems

Martin Connolly

eternal thanks !
Martn.

Snowchild Press, Ireland

Snowchild Press, Ireland
First Edition

ISBN-13: 978-1911100041
ISBN-10: 1911100041

Acknowledgement: 'The Snowchild', adapted from a medieval fabliau, appeared in North Magazine in Ireland in 1987. 'listening to rain' & 'commuter' appeared in English & in Japanese translation (by Yokota Mieko) in Tokyo-based tanka journal 'Sara' in 2006, respectively Aug & Sept issues.

Contents

la luna vino a la fragua

yardsticks

for Jim

first to ten
best of three
to hit either
of twin planks

upright fingers
breaking through
a carpet of water-

how many rocks
passed between-

none
probably
had that been
the game-

great salt bites
out of one

both
impeccably scarred-

considering sea
and middle age

half-defiant
rather than
half-eaten

The Snowchild

Wife waved husband goodbye.
Leaves curled, like old men's fists,
the woman returned to her shack.
The grass yellowed, the sun fell.
Winter, circling like a bird,
preyed on skin, and loneliness.
Clouds turned colic, coughing
rain, and later snow.

Two years passed, the man returned,
driving wealth before him,
with whistle and birch. Wife
and a new baby looked on.

'Where did he spring from?'
the man asked.

'From my womb,' she answered.
'I went walking at winter.
A snowflake fell onto my
tongue and I conceived.'

'I have calved too,' said
the man over the noise
of his herd.

Leaves unfurled and greened
once more, old trees turned
new planks, and built a home
where the shack had stood.
Summer resumed, the markets began,
and wife urged husband
to love her son, to take him
to see the market's fair.

Gladly he complied, and led
the little hand away
and never back.

'Where is my little snowflake
son?' cried the wife.

'I was careless,' the man
retorted. 'I held him up
to the sun, and he was gone.'

Cats

You liked cats. I liked cats.
I liked that you liked cats.
They were always a safe bet
for a gift, whether on a postcard,
or in 3d, like the Egyptian one
I was assured by a Luxor trader
was antique. He repeated the word
several times until I got the message.
I passed the lie together with the cat onto you.

Cats played a major role in your
film-noir of all-things-feminine.
The cast included an array of individualized
appurtenances: fingerless gloves, unmatched earrings
fragrances that denoted you when you were off-stage.
Your hair had a thousand faces.
Lighting was controlled by the tone of your voice.
Clothes were everything. Cats were everything.
It all remained cinema while I suspended disbelief.

However, my liking for these creatures never
really strayed beyond a timorous acceptance
of their unfathomable and unnerving constant swing
between indifference and affection.
It's now my policy not to scold the dog
when he tears off down the street
in hot pursuit of some cat -for two reasons:
(a) it's only show, a ritual he must preserve,
if nothing else, to show that he's a dog,
and (b) it demonstrates a healthy disrespect

I lacked.

July in Glengormley

The neighbours were all out.
Drums carried in on the wind.

Trebly, whistled versions
of British war-tunes

trickled
down

and gathered
with the steady toll

of Sunday bells
in a slough of sound.

Valley Park

I awoke to the sight of a ship
in the Lough, mutating, elongating
itself, until two ships
had unravelled, drifting apart like debris.

I lay back on the grass, unsure
that I had really been asleep, my mind
locked into a repetitive word-tag
of dandelion, dent-de-lion, daisy, day's

eye, like a deliberate block to thought
-or the image of you being led
away, your own eye opened up
obscenely, following me still.

An image

of calm water. A pocket by the edge
of some unnamed, unanswered lake
reflects my hand almost perfectly,

in retrospect at least. Then, a moment
later, the palm undulates-
the image warps as the air stirs.

Before long I will set up all the gear,
the line, the complicated reel, the pellet weights,
and wince to fit the solitary worm
I fished out of the earth behind me
on the hook. Alternatively,

all this will be done for me.
When I cast I will catch nothing.

Now a pocket torch is making circles
on the larger stones, adumbrating
surfaces within the whole, for study.
Here, a glint of silver throws the light
back through a sheen of underwater dust.

For the first few moments
the lake is not allowed to grow
beyond my chosen square foot
of rocks and water.
I make the most unlikely angler.

A larger ripple, mothered by a landing swan
perhaps, a flock of them, some way out,
breaks over my cramped shoes.
If it's noticed, and it is,
the paternal admonition comes. The memory ends.

The image of the water stays,
resisting, quietly, all the definitions
I will place upon it.

The details vary, like a lie,
with each new telling to myself.
One suggests the other, in some effete
conspiracy to get it right.
It needn't be like this, but

the quiet moment of that beauty,
be it memory or a yearning,
will not go unadorned for very long.

The Helicopters

The sound of helicopters circling
doesn't necessarily offend us less
or accord with any sense of
what's being done is being done for us
and any inconvenience caused is worth it.
It's simply not the daily problem here.
We don't need constant watching
or to be labelled 'scum'
like the people of West Belfast
to be part of it.
The violence on the screen
upsets us more, much more, than, say,
the discovery of a pubic hair
in the morning cup of coffee.
Indeed, on certain days
we're deafened by the roar of helicopters
as the Royals fly in
and over our estate.
Normally, however, they're
silent, evanescent things,
that dart and swim about far-off,
like tadpoles,
on the greying backdrop of a zinc sky.

listening to rain

rain simmered evenly
and temperately
and undramatically
at first,
at least
until
the drains
and accidental troughs
had grown fat
on water-

attention-seeking
endomorphic second
generation raindrops
began to leap
at random
near and far
onto stone
and leaf
and concrete,
imparting depth
by sacrifice-

but then,
as if to punish
or erase the memory

of these watery suicides
an angry-sounding
wall of water
fell, and
re-established
uniformity-

the noise eclipsed
the passing trains,
the neighbours
and the CD player-
thousands
in their millions
fell,
and the earth
grew sodden
where they lay-

historians
and naturalists
were not surprised,
however,
when it all
dried up
en masse,
and fearless
if now not-quite-so-
endomorphic raindrops
began
to leap
again

Cartoon

Chopping cookies the other day
the blade absolutely baulked.
Heads popped out of it
and gloved hands, punching
through each side, held
each one as each one screamed
and hollered stop and
don't let's do this anymore.

With practiced showmanship,
spreadeagled on the chopping board,
the reprieved cookie
scooped the sweat from
his brow and whistled phew.

Encouraged and emboldened,
the others, bleary-eyed
amidst the ruins of themselves,
scrambled into action,
and crumbs ran round
with trumpets egging on
the cookies' bits and pieces
to pull themselves together.

But some were slow, unwilling
and resigned to fate-
and had grown moustaches-
and, anyway, just when
it looked as though

one brave cookie
had rejourneyed back into itself
something stirred within
the nearby porcelain bowl.

Spouting out about
its rights of destiny
the cake mixture reared
imperiously, treacly hands
on treacly hips, casting
dark and dangerous stares
down upon the disarray
and shrieked don't
you even think about it,
just un-whole yourself
once more again and
buckle down, and take it
like a man.

And, of course,
the cookies, cookies being timid
at the best of times,
scattered back into
their crumbled, chopped existence.

The mixture to the blade
announced, unfunnily,
you may proceed.

Second Attempt, on the train back from Fuji
November 2nd, '93

The trains:
my journeys-
spaghetti lines to Fuji,

approach to Kawaguchiko
a window-full
of Fujimolgy

resplendent, crafted
computer-enhanced,
eyes enlarged

but Kawaguchiko
is bored
with Fuji.

Autumn-blackened,
tourist-beaten,
empty plates of faces.

And, yesterday, excited,
then let down,
today warily enthused

I caught the 10.05
right up her
-into nothing,

a viewing pen,
two thousand metres up
fifty metres wide,

nowhere wild to roam
my eyes champed on
above's meagre Fuji ration:

dog-biscuit peak,
head-shot from behind
of a coal lump,

below, the mists
are fake, stolen
from the postcards

and by this stage
I am ready
to utter choice expletives.

To top this
the 11.30 (rescue) bus
pisses off at 11.15.

Five hours' journey (twice),
the perfect flattery,
perfectly ignored.

Already, though,
the mythopoesis
is off and

marching with me,
down in seconds flat:
9 kms in 1 hour 15,

purpose drawn

from train times,
forward movement

the indelible roundness
of doing exactly
as much as you can,

what I told myself,
a camera for protection
beneath the giant form.

What I'll tell others,
who couldn't know,
eloquent pauses

which, in time,
even I will find mystery in.

Eating an apple on a commuter train in Japan

I'm wondering
are they wondering
what I'm going to
do with this
humungous Japanese apple
now that I'm
nearing its
prodigious core-

but I only have
an audience
of one:
a girl's
infant eyes
locked studiously
onto so rare
a sight-

will you go
the whole hog,
they ask,
and make it
disappear,
or slip
the sordid remnant
into some unlikely
resting place:
rucksack pouch,
trouser pocket,
sweaty palm?

Down to nibbling
now, my eyes
negotiate:
if I make it
disappear
will you fall
off your seat
in wonderment,
or tug your
mother's sleeve
and point?

It all ends
disappointingly:
I pop the whole hog core
into my mouth
and champ
on seed and
vegetated gristle
before
unwidened eyes-

she turns away
and looks about
the carriage:

without my apple
I am unremarkable.

labournight

for Meg

(26/27 January 1996, Kyodo Hospital, Isehara, Japan)

you were immobilised
with pain
but I was hungry,
so I ate-

for once
at least
I could give you
some real-time feedback
on the fruits
of your daily labour

praising the shiitake
and the al dente rice-

grafting normality
onto the anything but-

because this
was the other kind
of labour,
and it felt strange-

strange to be here,
to have stolen out
of work

and to see you
on the sofa where
we'd eaten breakfast

only hours before

immobilised and almost
mute with pain-

strange to know
this was the moment
our life changes-

so I followed
the followable,
and ate

....

I emptied
the camera bag
and filled it

panic-grabbing
CDs and apple
and water
and *Pregnancy
and Childbirth-*

weeks of handling
had dampened
the initial shock
of its graphic
monochrome shots

-the close-up birthings
sweated hair
and blood,
and naked grimaced faces

now familiar to us–

and it didn't try
to tell us
the pain is not pain
as *The Well Pregnancy
Book* had–

your body
was shuddering
with the newness
of a pain
it had never felt–

I was thinking
of hospital policy,
how to fill time

in some nearby corridor
barred from
being with you

when I packed
the *Collected Stories
of Philip K Dick*–

they had told me
repeatedly no
you cannot attend

and I believed them
so I put in PKD
and hoped

I'd have visions
of starways
and cold matter

colliding with alien
craft, driven
by plot-driven characters

pursuing ideas
to keep me awake,
and assuage me

in my separation
from you,
and your pain-

Beyond Lies the Wub,
and beyond lay
the womb

and our child
with his/her hands
flat together

pointing downward,
ready to dive

....

the surface
was uninviting-
brown leather

taut as a drum,
surrounding walls
and glass cabinets

aged and bleak,

the room echoed
hollowly of pain-

dulled chrome contraptions,
some with tubes
some with wires

loitered
motionless
in the functional room-

it took us a while
to figure it out,
or perhaps it was

a resistance mechanism
telling us the delivery room
couldn't be like this-

you had drawn
a plan of the ward
and tagged each room
in readable romaji-

the *shussan no heya*
was the adjoining room
only yards away

but distance was governed
by a new physics-

the slow, exacting
science of dilatation-

vacant beds either side,
we were alone
in the *jintsu no heya*-

with its sharp nasal pinch
in the middle, *jintsu*
conveyed more pain
than 'contractions'

but they were
coming in a language
beyond words-

....

the book told me
what to do
and you refined it

gasping commands
as my hands burrowed
into your lower back

and agony spread
its black wings
through you-

initially I couldn't do
the sympathetic
breathing thing-

it required
a step beyond
my awkward first self

still floundering in
questions

and concern-

it took a while
to go beyond
my visitor persona

half an hour at least
or until the arrhythmic
rhythms of contractions

had broken me up
broken up unusedness
or until

you said
please speak
and left it wide

enough for banalities
and discrete bits
to be enough-

....

placeless muzak
off-white walls
ancient posters
Victoriana beds-

one of them
had to go-

I stuck on
Fresh Takes
and suddenly

the place
was ours-
reels and hornpipes
were soothing
to you-

two years previous
and I'd be
pissed or stoned
listening to this,
Nirvana and
Bob Dylan-

Bo and I
drinking out
the night
enjoying and lamenting
our unfixedness

words in free fall
time in free fall-

until right now
beneath the double clock
of minutes and centimetres-

both spread out
like rumours of themselves
and like rumours
only teased-

the midwives came
and went- gently
softly, caringly,
disappointing us-

'not yet'

became shorthand
for not for ages yet-

a small bloom
of blood and issue
on your gown
mixed the strands
of hope and fear-

for nine months
the child had been
a part of you-

two biologies in one

the inseparable
now outliving itself
maturing into
two

the child
wanting to be

gravitating
to the music
and the light
the voices
and the mystery
of its limbs

landlocked still
within the
too-familiar-

mother and child
yearned for
a new relationship

and respective
curiosities assuaged
the waves of fire-

the wickerwork of muscles
was working through you
relentlessly-

....

I packed in anecdotes
between each agony

the one
where I spend the night
in a phone booth in Cornwall

and call the operator
for a chat, someone
to talk to

and then it starts

the one
where I'm in a train compartment
with a would-be wanna-be IRA man

his face pushed into mine
acting out his good cop,
bad cop routine-

again

the one
where me and Domhnall
are navigating to our tent

through a pitch-black Aran night
half-cut on Baileys
and stumble on the Provies selling guns

your hand grips mine

the one
where Jim and me
get into running

to shake the cobwebs,
release an endorphin or two,
and run round a bloody mountain

starting…

the one
where I'm smoking King Edwards
in another pitchblack Irish night, with Pedro

swapping tales of apparitions
and *fuegos fatuos*
issuing from graves-

no words

the one
where I play guitar in public
and the Ma drinks me under the table

your sudden cry

the one

where I nearly disappear
in an Irish bog

again…

the one
where I'm arrested
for getting my head kicked in

-which I almost told
locked into autobio mode
listening to myself-

the one
where I am six
it's a white Christmas

and we've made a train of chairs
in the living-room

and we are happy
because we are loved and
unaware of pain-

your face would tighten
suddenly and each memory
would end where it was

no hope to return
to finish, embellish, extrapolate
and no desire either-

because with each memory
finished another step
towards transition-

a word I taught you

quoting from the book
to wrap your pain in science

and to ignore the clock
which had already spelt out
ten hours of this-

ten hours
in this otherwise unoccupied
unadorned maternity ward

ten hours
of contractions
surging through you

ten hours
of you
listening to me-

transition was the realm
where eight centimetres
would blossom into nine, ten

and it beckoned
as a purpose
in all this-

time was pain
expanding sharply
by degrees-

....

appropriately
around the graveyard hour

of four

the ghost of Tom Joad
appeared, and Springsteen
sang our disappointment
for us-

the pin-drop silence without
pressed in upon us both-

....

by six
I had my chance
to delve into those
starways and cold matter-

I was
asked to leave
and did
and brought PKD
with me
and the rest
still packed into
the camera bag-

but I couldn't read
or avail of any of whatever
distractions I had
because I was
exhausted and operating
on the basis of immediate
and simple perception
like looking down
at the slippers on my feet

40

and noting their
off-whiteness as
essential to their being
and more important
than whatever purpose
they could otherwise
have been designed to serve-

and down the corridor
wondering would
they let me join you
in the delivery room
and what beauty
resided in the stillness
of hospitals at dawn
and was I ready
or would I be so upset
if they said no
and what it might be like
to actually witness
the birth
and that I was
potentially
terrified-

and that
when eventually
they relented
on hospital policy
and told me
I could join you
I was indeed
terrified,
but not only-

....

something of my awkward
first self reappeared briefly
seeing you on the delivery bed
machines and cabinets stocked
with calibrated jars
all around you-

the intimacy of the labour room
was gone

the midwives had lost
their unrushed softness
and were fixing things

my anecdotes
had outlived themselves

now
I was unsure
what to say-

unfazed
your eyes
smiled at me

seeing only
you and I-

plan A
fell completely flat
and my hand with it

after ten minutes under you
what it lost in blood
it gained in comic effect-

it imparted at least
a touch of sympathetic pain
to add to the fatigue

which of course
was nil compared
to yours

significant only
as something
we shared

where sharing
was completely
utterly significant-

only now
seventeen hours on
since I left for work

and you said
don't worry
it won't be today

seventeen hours
of your muscles
clasping into you

uterine cells in millions
tensing up in rings
working from the top

and passing down
through *increment* and *acme*
dispensing torment

unimpressed and undeterred
by pain or screams
leaving you each time

debilitated
shocked
relieved

only now
were you allowed
to push

only now
the conscious
and the autonomic

melded

and you
could join in actively
the child's irresistible dream

of breaking out-

and I could
hold you
touch you

soothe your
burning forehead
with damp cloth

hope with you
breathe with you
push with you

at least

in breaths
(plan B)-

....

one hour on however
familiar disappointment
drifted back

this time minus Springsteen
and for some time
minus midwives and the doctor-

descent was not occurring
and another birthing mother
had arrived, and got priority

in the adjoining theatre-
in lieu, we had
the fetal monitor

consoling us with science
tracking heartrates
feeding out the jagged highs

and lows,
uninterpretable
and unstoppable-

the unknowns
and unknowables
were building up

and the repertory
of optimism

was wearing thin-

the air was filled
with alternating
focused screams

midwives, gaily, almost,
encouraging
a sense of competition-

'ganbatte!'
handclaps, laughter
shouted soothing words-

at seven fortyish
the birth scream happened
-in the other room-

our unborn child
could hear
a just-born's cries

a new sound
thrown into
the vision of beyond

a different kind of scream
vigorous in its helplessness-

....

exhaustion had claimed
your body
disenfranchised it of power-

the contractions
torturing you
hardening your face

into taut lines
were simply not strong enough
the midwife said-

they'd fitted up
a drip of
pinkish stuff

to induce,
notching up the flow
as the unmorning dragged on-

but it hadn't touched
the rest of you-
exhaustion, pain

were out of the equation
of persistence, fight,
and love-

will
immoveable
empowered you-

kept you clear
and us
tight-

passing over
your mother tongue
choosing mine

-ours-

to keep me
with you-

but I didn't
have your strength-

exhaustion
was walking
all over me-

loosening
my balance,
affording glimpses of collapse

tempting me
with the notion
of escape-

the subterfuge
of needing to wet
the cloth for your forehead
seemed the most
convincing-

my first attempt
failed in the shock
of your voice-

but ten minutes on
I'd given up on
not giving in

and I turned
away and
ran-

back into

the labour room

transformed
by morning sun

into the ordinary-

all three beds
made up, pristine-

I shot into
the ward's bathroom
and lashed my face
with full-force tap water
uttering what I needed to
to bathe myself in
my own weakness
before I could be strong again-

and doing this
I could return
(not forgetting to wet the cloth)-

by eightish
the doctor had decided
it was time

to speak beyond
the echo of the midwives'
'mada, mada', not yet, not yet-

his calm stirred
only slightly
as he searched around

his what was probably much-
uncalled-for skill

in English

and
came up with
'fetal distress'

sown
with all the care
and the precision

necessary
to impart
gravity without shock-

he had
the face for it-
unperturbable and humorous

(and beyond that
somehow he resembled
Tezuka Osamu

creator of Leo
cartoon legend
of a white lion

strange because that same Leo
was the name we'd chosen
if our child would be a boy)-

the kindness
of his effort to explain
struck me first

before the vague
implications of 'fetal distress'
could insinuate themselves

into the palpable
form of my own
growing distress-

fear held back
in the chamber
of the unspoken

until now-

the doctor
next produced
a vacuum extractor

which I either
didn't see or my memory's
chosen to delete-

I wiped your forehead
touched you, held you
inhaled, exhaled

in perfect time with you
spat out words
of love at you

poured out sweat
with you, shook
and shuddered with you

screamed with you

and suddenly
the air was busy
with the imminence

of birth-

the midwife placed her hands
at the top of the abdomen
and pushed rudely down

with all her weight
to force the baby out

while the doctor
and the other midwife
pulled-

and I looked
first at you

because I'd heard
a new cry

which spoke
all my fear for me

rude articulation
of the possibility

of death
as well as life

pure, simple
unadorned-

I turned
and saw

down below
the sheets

a brownish
rubbery body

had appeared
into the waiting hands-

the doctor pronounced
the child 'otokonoko'

and my mind
juggled its meaning

between boy and girl
unable to decide-

reason, thought
suspended-

in those two or
three seconds

I had seen enough-
looked back to you

your eyes
focused over us

staring at a point
above us, beyond us

your body
pulsating

rapid
short gasps

issuing,

hyperbreathing-

I watched helpless
terrified

alone
before you-

until the breathing
reached its peak

began
to ebb

and the knowable
returned

and you
returned to you-

I could touch you
hold you, kiss you

cry with you
and all in triumph

unalloyed euphoria-
'a boy', you clarified

Elegy for a Convenience Store

Miserably
a year or so ago
our beloved 7-11
packed up on us
and died-

beloved
because it fit
the perfect ideal
of convenience-

so close
we called it
our refrigerator-

it had hit upon
hard times, it seemed,
and fell into
an unannounced decline

unnerving us precisely
for being unannounced-

the shelves' impoverishment
grew by day and night
in mystery-

the magic cornucopia
that restocked the shelves invisibly
was gone-

in its place
prosy neon-basted shadows
wallowed slothfully
in the widening
empty spaces-

knock-down price-
tags suddenly appeared
like mold
on cereal packs
and last year's
plastic toys-

overnight
the staff's manner
had shifted down a key
below the line
of acceptable engagement-

eye-contact
had been cut-

the obligatory welcomes
were unkissed by humour,
even good humour

faces fallen, knit
into the energy-conserving
moroseness of a caretaker's-

the giant floor-cleaner
in the graveyard-shift
sucked up

more attention
than the customers received-

by day
my steps beyond
the formulaic
silence of the customer
drew gaping blanks-

hello was answerless,
irrelevant-

and
so was I,
unfaced money-
tenderer,

identity reduced
to the bar-code
on my yoghurt tub-

then one Sunday
the world fell in
or so it must have seemed
to the staff-member
locked into that slo-
mo entropy-

a lady backed her car
-too far-
into the display window
causing heads to turn
and shards to spill
onto the soft-porn mags
the hard linoleum
and the concrete-

there was no rush
to fix it
beyond a simple brush-up
and a tape-job-

so it languished
for a week,
an abject ruin
of its former self

until D-day
when the shutters
shut, and
all the lights
were stopped-

in its place we've got
a curtain shop
which no-one goes to-

we play
spot-the-customer
as we walk by
and no-one ever wins-

now we have to walk
two full minutes more
to hit the next
convenience store-

negotiate
two traffic lights

double-check
for drunken drivers,

and,

the bread is different-

memory's hung
a string of leaden pellets
around our feet-

only sometimes,
say, on an emergency
milk and choux crème run,

does one
fall off
and trickle
miserably
away

and the inconvenience
of former glories
dies a
little

bit

with

it

for Leo, at eighteen months
(August '97)

bu burgeoned into *ba*
which developed into *bai*
and wandered here and there
until it found its echo
and evolved into a binary,
bai bai-

and meaning grew with it-

leavings summoned *bai*
byes in profusion-
absence followed
in their wake-
the bilabial butterflies
burrowed into consciousness-

the sound of what
cannot be changed,
sound of our own
powerlessness

could only be defeated
by its own acquisition-

now our child

61

throws bye bye back at us
whenever it suits him-

bye bye
when it's Sunday morning
and no-one's going anywhere-

bye bye
when he's ate his fill
and now it's time to play-

bye bye
in mid-hug, just to hear
it is indeed not bye bye-

it is bound up
with his observation
of the world-

there are no inanimate,
insensate objects
in the world-

bye bye
to little friends
in Shimobara park

bye bye
to the express train
rushing in the distance

bye bye
to car and bus and motorbike
random on the street

and bye bye
only under protest

to the miraculous moon

inextinguishable
by curtains, cloud,
his parents' myths-

and as there are no
inanimate, insensate objects
in the world

nor are there
sights which offend
or displace curiosity-

as we ambled through
the veggie plots
at the back of us
under the warming
morning sun
I swallowed my distaste
and followed
his sudden intent gaze

and to
a dying worm
being plundered
by ants,
innumerable and tiny,
body curling
only slowly
he uttered sweetly
almost sadly
bye bye

for Ken, at nineteen months

hardly awake
you're already curious,
drawn to the window
to check the outside
is still there-

only yesterday: a prospect of coats,
air thickened with winter coughs,
the hiss of the hydraulic doors
and the ringing of mobiles-

your smile draws me in
to your curiosity-
and I am like you,
amazed at the street below
in its ordinariness-

a tinny disembodied voice
tells the stations out
like water marks, feeding
their importance to us-

64

you point at a passerby,
then point at the window-lock,
and your eyes turn to me
pointedly saying
open it, please-

beside me a head
falls on my shoulder
lolling fitfully back
only after my indignant nudge-

the adult in me
says 'it's too cold'
and 'you've only just woken',
and then the you in me
undoes the latch-

with a banshee roar
our mirror-image flashes past
shattering the windows'
peace, and mine-

as the offending glass goes
the image of outside
takes its first breath
capturing you
with its freedom all-

disgorged onto the platform
suddenly exhausted and relieved,
out of one creaking mechanism
and into my own-

now you're talking,
letting out your joy

and naming things,
throwing out a greeting
to another passerby-

a thousand of us
unconnected souls
flowing in unison
under girders and the clock-

the thousand leaves
of that bright gingko
grab us both,
golden, fragile, framed
beneath a paper-tear sky-

divergence finds its pattern
and our footsteps grow
into a hollow thunder,
falling into place-

and each leaf finds its freedom
back-slapped by the wind
and each one in return
dances to the earth-

and you are with me
in that place
I've fallen into
and we are dancing,

boyo-

Busker, Grafton Street

I'm just past Bewley's
and it starts distantly
to beat its idea out
beyond itself and through the street
into the folds of Quality Control
snaked within my head-

we're suitably impressed
but some among us
are dismissing it as artificial-
Yamaha's new rhythm box
piped through Aria's new amp-
now where's the fun in that?

alternatively, it might be all preamble
to some power chords and sax,
an ensemble, with printed name
and twelve homegrown CDs
arrayed before the inevitably-black-
sunglassed guitarist's open case-

on approach, the critics silence
and converge, in a kind of awe-
to see the band contracted and condensed
into a single seated figure
rapping two empty plastic bottles
on his very ordinary lap-

machine-precision beats
pulsed and layered and over-lapped

and played with, toyed around-
the player rocking slowly,
succumbing to the total rhythm-
and his audience is growing-

the applause is growing in my head,
I'm speechifying in my speechlessness
on the player's 'perfect efforts'
'mining his taut being',
'so much with so little'
and stuff like that-

we've had a whip-round,
all the senses chipping in
to turn the 50p into a pound
no less -my contribution buys me
a private audience, a question,
the right to vocalize some praise-

for free, a drunken girl berates
'You make all this?
Just for hitting these wee bottles?
I could fuckin' do that myself-
Away on!' and her friend drags her on-
the player looks the other way-

musculature and mind all
given over to his next performance-
as I move on I look the other way
of a distant disappointment
hearing the same rhythm beat out-
routine in among the wonder-

copper mug

at the centre
of his makeshift world
with its longitude and latitude
of drying underthings,
heaped molasses blankets
dulled all out of colour,
where weather systems
hesitate before
the self-made wall-less space,
his pristine copper mug
is quietly outré-
the lion on its dimpled sides
comes off at night
and will not let him sleep-

commuter

my fingers stall above the coins
against the flow of bodies
and the morning at my back-

like some lost memory resurfacing
the newly-minted sits among the dull-

like my first day at school
among the unknown others
I'd have one new thing

always in my hand,
the newness rubbing off with sweat-

my attention-grabber, reality-displacer-
but back then my movements
were all awkward and unlearnt,

now I have my choreography down
learning from my silent peers-

so when the 7.32 rolls in
I never feel quite so bad, or so undignified
scrummaging for a seat,

the coin pristine, lodged
within my commuter's soul-

State of the Union

it must be very nice to get applauded
when you pause, not to mention the relief
that inevitably attends the heightened moment
when you stop and silence fills you up-
big words need such audience support
or else, God (in Whom We Trust) forbid,
they might fall flat, like clutched-at straws,
or a first year's nervous utterances,
all awkward, thick, and simple-

but though they seem to like him,
their constant, orchestrated claps obtrude,
like periodic bursts of static
chopping up the eloquence
of a Christian Sunday radio recital-

oh let him speak! an urge within me says,
'truth' and 'freedom' do not need support-
the giant constructs of community
can stand unaided in the silence,
bare, uncomplicated, weighty-

a million tons of meaning on a stick, perhaps,
like something out of Dali,
but yet it can be done-
so let him speak and let the words
stand clear, unbloodied,
radiant and bone-white clean-

and whatever silences remain
you will simply have to live with,
die with,
kill with,
lie with

l'enfer

after
aggressive drunken businessman
terrifies passengers at station
delays the 16.46
is carried off by three officials
had to be restrained
was gone
we dutifully resumed
our previous positions,
faces,
stances,
parts-

and while some stolen glances
intimated shared experience,
some momentary lapse
into community,
no-one spoke-

the '46 rolled out at '51
as quietly as it had arrived

and our bodies lolled upon the platform
counting down the seconds to the '54

while overhead, unseen
the display had fallen into idle mode
playing out its streaming comic-strip
of tiny orange bulbs
about unattended bags,
suspicious packages etc

somehow, gently,
gently, gently
mocking us

poster

a quiet uncovering-
unrushed delicacy-
a theatre of nylon mesh and skin
stares down-

the eyes
inquisitive
and probing,
silent,

hand upon
another's hair
is making up
for speech-

the unsaid
sanctity of touch
is coursing in
and out of words

lulling as the motion
of the carriage,
into a dark continuum-
the fishnet-stocking universe

is prey to warps,
and even tears
in its own fabric-
as when

the sliding doors tear open
and a gaggle of aging geese
in necklaces and purple hair and hats
wade in, and cackle up a riot

Sicilian hitman

the monotony of building-scapes
and watching others sleep
can overwhelm-

only arrival
or some sudden jolt, calamity
or the boarding of new blood

can shake
the mental processes
out of their descent-

for 'new blood' read sexy,
interesting, unconventional, loud, obnoxious,
or even sinister-

the Sicilian hitman-type, for example, might make it on
just as the doors are sliding shut-
anyone else doing it inevitably will flap

feel the need to give some signal,
an embarrassed cough, perhaps,
to acknowledge the intrusion

but not the hitman type-
a sideways step
from one reality to ours

he enters
as though he was always there,
half-human, half-revealed religion-

those who notice him
may be converted unto wakefulness
by his eyes alone

classically cold
unblinking and disinterested,
stage-direction perfect

lost upon a middle distance
of braided crops
barely moving in the daytime heat-

the poster fifteen feet away he glances at occasionally
is in his reality a whitewashed shack
upon a sunbrowned hill

where he will go
with his *9mm Tanfolglio T95*,
a name and face to match-

of course it's all a fallacy-
a real Sicilian hitman you wouldn't see
until the leaden zero of a barrel's end

appeared before your eyes-
a moment only to purvey the holder's
business-like grin, just out of focus-

that poor, unsmiling man is probably very nice-
his eyes just telling us he's tired,
that he's done this journey ten thousand times-

at worst he hates his boss-
has even contemplated shooting him,
fleetingly, half-jokingly-

his mind is on his family awaiting him, perhaps,
oblivious to all
and casually contemptuous with it

his vacant gaze
into the middle distance
a protest at the city gnawing at his soul-

that, or possibly he will indeed
kill someone-
maybe even me

astronomy

I watched two stars from my window last night
they kind of tricked me into prolonging closing the shutters
froze me where I stood
as neighbours sometimes do
talking about the weather or the lateness of the rubbish truck

they flickered on and off
which may sound a little strange
but not really
not when I tell you I would block one out and then the other
by squinting overly

I do that sometimes
even scrunch my face up like a kid
who won't be told
and has just learned the value of being naughty
pulling faces and making funny noises

of course they flickered also because they're stars
and their journey to the eye is over
a little turbulence is only to be expected
six thousand years one seemed to say
a million raised the other

vying for attention
the attention
of an Earthling in pyjamas
at a window
getting cold

at Hotel New Akao

Co-ordinates:
I'm lounging over-comfortably
on a vaguely Louis Quatorze armchair
precisely where the corridors converge
on the fourth floor of **Hotel New Akao,**
Atami, Shizuoka, Japan-

I stretch my left arm out unhurriedly
and rest it on the elaborate wooden crest
of the adjacent matching sofa
as my right hand probes
the textures of my hat-

if someone comes they'll see
a man at one with himself
at home and unabashed
relaxing midst the quiet
of this cavernous edifice
undetermined and intent upon very little

taken possibly with the fluctuating whirrs
and micro-shakes and rattles
of the vending machine on his right-

last night he drank two thirds
of a bottle of Georges Duboeuf Beaujolais
four cans of Asahi Super Dry
and the contents of a hipflask
filled with Whitehorse Scotch
sneaked into the sea-level dining-room
and transferred slug-by-slug

into the otherwise innocuous glass of water
and ice before him at the family table-

he calls this normal
or at best a metaphor for bad behaviour
his controllable excess-

he worries only what the evening's intake
has done to his waistline
and will all that day's photos
show him with a double-chin-

he's prey to cyclical behaviour
patterned steps and missteps
that unfold their own long corridor of doors
and random oases of inviting furniture
micro-quaking drink dispensers
the footfalls of the odd guest here and there
or a hotel staff who smiles
and breaks the quiet with a gentle
hayo go zaimasu-

the 'I' is here
her greeting reassures me
it's taking stock
listening to the hum and whirr
of my own middle age
behatted
stationary
interminably
drifting
lounging
slouching
falling

Remembering Giant's Causeway,
at Dōgashima, 2008

and the Ma
quite understandably
as a wall of North Atlantic Ocean
broke in front of us
noticing my entrancement asked
well are you inspired yet, boyo?

the moment flashes back
as a hundred feet below
a different ocean breaks...

the thickened glass
has killed the sound of wind and wave
and I am quite alone

cut off suddenly from joy
I see you in your bed which 'breathes'
to combat bedsores

and I know you will not sit again
beside the great Atlantic
not clamber over to the Wishing Chair

and I will not have to answer
your very understandable inquiry
with my complicatedness

it's not like that
not quite like that
I said looking at the great waves
crashing mercilessly and grandly
and wordlessly
before us

when 'yes' was all it took

baguette

with stealth
disguised as nonchalance
intent
dressed up as vacancy
subject A
entered Saint Germain
and found
precisely what he'd come
looking for

and only one remained

with panic
pretending to be care
haste
in pins and rollers
subject A
manipulated tongs
as focused
as an astronaut
in space

and placed upon the tray his prize

waltzing
on his unseen cloud
across
that final aching gap
between
his modest dream
of lunch
and sweet fulfillment
he landed it

ah, but then a baker passed

five practiced fingers
held up
a tray of fresh baguettes
wafting
out unconscious taunts
at subject A
to abandon that old
hardened
morning-heavy stick

which, of course, made A reflect

it preyed upon
his fragile joy
and filled him
with an angst
in miniature
a tiny sound
of broken glass
and sighs
awakening

and yet he reached into his pocket

obedient
to the smiling counter lady
and the role
he was locked into
entreaties
not to tamper
with delight
whatever shape
it just might take

Family Holiday

Today we are in the Vosges,
the Vosges,

partly buoyed
and partly sunk

by road signs
wrapped in mystery

and houses coyly
sheltered

succumbing to the trees
and climbing banks

and absent sounds
that shout

the Vosges, the Vosges

its sea of deep green
branching round us
whispering, crowding, nudging
welcoming us with the gossip
of its leaves and boughs

the *sotto voce* Vosges
is calling out to me-

we have stopped for petrol
and the smell of petrol

father's shirtless body,
wielding petrol-gun and francs
as the August rain sheets down
into this mountain sauna-

the 40s petrol-pump
reminds me of a joke at school
take me to your leader
take me to your leader
bleats the alien to the pump

as rivulets of rain snake across the windows
warping all the edges
of the little mountain garage
moulding all the wood
and rusted corrugated iron
into something equally as organic
as the crowding trees-

the petrol mixes with the remnant
of Ma's last cig
look at yon, she says with scorn
look at the gut on that,
the bloody eejit's no sense

as the bloody eejit
fights the summer storm and saves the day

spluttering out his *merci beaucoups*
to the beret-wearing man-

he gets inside and with the usual battering
and suppressed expletives

in the presence of a minor
off we go again
into the Vosges
into the Vosges-

the alien
has entered too

frustrated by the pump
giving all humanity
one last chance to speak
it sits beside me
as we tear on

and they tear on in front
in their own half-hearted *sotto voce* words

and I despair,
imagining, quite rightly,
that enough of this
will only lead to more frustration

when absent sounds
turn up in all ugliness

and even, dare I think it,
wrapped within my own half-mystery,
invite some cataclysmic end

amid the softness
and delicious longeur

of the Vosges, the Vosges,
the Vosges

the Vosges

announcement

passengers are advised,
due to a tear in the space-time continuum
on the Keihin-Tohoku Line,
of possible disruption-

trains are liable
to traverse distances in no time at all
resulting in inevitable anteriorities
and likely periods of great inaction-

magazines and other reading material
will be provided, where possible and according to supply,
to ease the passage of time
and/or dampen any sense of emptiness or incipient alienation-

passengers may experience return
to a point earlier in the day or week
and are asked to comply with whatever repetition is required
in order not to change the course of history-

Keihin-Tohoku is not liable
for expenses or emotional damage
but will issue official notification
stubs at the barriers-

passengers are also advised
not to leave clothes, toiletries or items of a highly personal nature
in the carriage upon disembarkation
as these may become improperly recycled or get lost in eternity-

service will be resumed as soon as possible:
trains are likely to be running normally
tomorrow, and for the foreseeable future and in perpetuity
of a general all-pervasive contrived sense of purpose and direction-

Encounter at Oyama, April 2012

an elegance in white had caught my eye
and so I stopped and stared at it
the cold of the mountain momentarily gone
the cold of just-seen death gone too
a crane

she stood on corrugated iron
the roof of an outhouse adjoining a yard and dwellings
taking careful tremulous steps
as though unwilling to create a stir
a sound

evacuated her bowels without a stir certainly
not a feather ruffled nor a hair out of place
I wondered were her feet strategically placed
to avoid all contact and keep her pristine and
aloof

soon she wandered down as only cranes can do
falling first then widening wings and cupping air
braking precisely at the moment to make a perfect shadow
on a patch of dry in the middle of the river
alone

or unaware of me at least because I had not moved
captive of the theatre of this sleek creature
her perfect silhouette of albumen or alabaster
framed by greens and browns and water flowing all
around

her delicacy against the rough and readiness of all
aristocratic poise without the aristocracy
unlearned inscaped sense of where to tread and how
sensitized to suddenness in the immediacy before her
alive

the thought occurred to me of course
about the soul betaking itself to heaven or wherever
and briefly showing up in some creature's perfect form
treading silently toward its silent shimmering
away

and yet with every step the crane was getting closer
picking out a convoluted route to me
stepping over stone and grass and flow
its bright white resolving into textures I could only now
appreciate

still ever delicate and poised
the supple arching neck reflexed now and then
as though indignant at the slightest waft and warp of air
her old world sensibilities on show
an actress

I did not move nor had I moved for ages
untouched by time the mountain chill
the need that drags us on with complicated reasons
thought invading action
and desire

alas of course it could not last
some sudden perturbation within her sight or sense
and off she flew back over the stream where she had wandered
away from where I stood a way a lone a last a loved
a long the

the curse

I knew I shouldn't curse the old dear in front and if I did I
soon replaced the thought
with some palliative reasoning to the effect I hadn't meant it
and one should respect
be flexible and suppress the kneejerk reflexes coming as they
do at every encounter
a million faces to contend with in a year of holding handrails
among strangers
not to mention all those steps at quarter walking speed
unnaturally deliberate
the lifting and the placing of the soles upon the bullion bars
in grey laid out below us
and if anybody asks my eyes will tell them I'm an individual
and this blankness
that looks out at you has been cultivated scrupulously and is
far from a generic trait

she walked so slowly I concluded in a second she was likely
doing this on purpose
to annoy and this in turn allowed me to leak out my
imprecation my momentary scorn
my sudden transformation into Harry Lime telling Joseph
Cotton in the Ferris wheel
just look down at them they're like ants in their tininess and
meaninglessness and so on
humans that is just getting in the way and if one can rise
above them so be it and such
at which point elements kicked in and took me by the
metaphoric arm suggesting
I might possibly have overstepped the mark and trodden on a
tenet of some global faith
that thing by which we gauge our civilization with its Pepsi
Cola ads and crucifixes

it can be difficult to be nice and inconspicuous at every turn
but Jesus knows I try
I told myself as I tried not to say that she offending obstacle
before me was a cow
and wouldn't she be better sat at home in front of the TV not
annoying others
blocking passage to the six oh four or more appropriately in a
field chewing at the green
and then I caught a glimpse of her or rather she emerged into
my peripheral vision she
strained face all intent upon the calculation of energy
expended energy required
energy remaining remaining distance to the steps the sound
of train approaching all
microadjusting ever as she factored in the crowd around her
and pain from stone in shoe

and as I passed I saw all this and had even made a
storyboard depiction of the two of us
my own face roughly drawn but expressive of a certain
evolving self-disgust regret
but helpless in that I wasn't going to do a Genevieve and stop
and throw the race
that I was on a mission I was headed down that staircase in
my mind already hurtling
aerodynamically for that window of opportunity those sliding
doors in mid-yawn
which salivated as my peers rubbed up against those full
retracted Indian rubber gums
I wasn't going to compensate for cursing that poor unsinning
elderly old dear
because when it came down to it commuters simply have to
live with their generic traits

and something has to go

things the short-term memory stores and files away
before your key unlocks the front door

how to perambulate the carriage of a moving train and not
fall onto seated passengers
how to radiate nonchalance when that same train or another
makes a sudden stop
how to type and send an email from your iPhone as you
negotiate the station stairs

another one of late is not a how but more a kind of recent
trend or idiosyncrasy
half a trick and half a way of throwing in a dash of me aged
five and unaware of trains
the rectitude required for smooth commuting and a blank
expression as necessity-

passing through the ticket barriers of late my body tilts to
either left or right
and brushes up against the aluminum sidings within that
rarefied space
which are also smooth, unyielding, as featureless as the inner
walls of autoclaves-

but 'brushes up against' conceals more than it reveals,
pointing to involuntary
when in fact it's more like something conscious if not entirely
conscious either
an autonomic gesture of the undead five-year-old who never
lost his love of slides-

as somehow he's -or I'm- careering down the slide again, a
weightless body in free fall
entrapped by gravity and momentum, helter-skeltering round
and down a heady spiral,
willing victim of the inescapable, a pendulum released
escaping from its drudgery etc-

all very well of course if you are indeed just five and not near
fifty, aware of adult poise,
the possibility that the man behind you might have noted
your slightly strange manoeuver
and matched it covertly with observances from the station
previous, very FBI-

then you're in trouble, in a world in which not only what you
do but how you do it counts-
as when the train does halt suddenly and more than
not pitching forward
it's not pitching forward without a hair falling out of place
that really matters

passing by the postered walls of glossy smiling faces wrapped
in cotton wool and light
as you, say, replay scenes from last night's dinner when you
shouted at your kids
or walk subsumed by grief for the beloved dead and dying
your face a sculptured calm-

of course how could it be otherwise a million of us breaking
down in tears
or laughing uncontrollably at some remembered joke or

succumbing to a fit of ire
thumping from behind the bloke in front who's in your way
on out the carriage door

so I suppose the childish pleasure I derive from my
momentary slides here and there
is not much more than me releasing me a little from his adult
drudgery of obligation
my fateful joining of the masses as we cavort and ramble up
and down the hilly stairs

running here and there and scrambling for a seat and
dropping things and reading
comics and looking into five by seven centimetre screens
where dragons flick their tails
where no-one really knows precisely where they are
or even cares

61732493R00058

Made in the USA
Charleston, SC
25 September 2016